The Word Is Life

An Anthology
Of Funeral Meditations

CSS Publishing Company, Inc.
Lima, Ohio

Library of Congress Cataloging-in-Publication Data

The Word is life : an anthology of funeral meditations.
    p.   cm.
  ISBN 1-55673-598-7
  1. Funeral sermons. 2. Sermons, American. I. C.S.S. Publishing Company.
BV4275.W67   1994
252'.1—dc20
                                      93-39596
                                           CIP

ISBN 1-55673-598-7
                        PRINTED IN U.S.A.

Table Of Contents

Foreword

As we prepared to embark on the eight-hour return trip home from our visit with my grandmother, she would often say, "You know, I don't say 'goodbye' anymore. I prefer to say 'auf Wiedersehen,' which means 'I will see you again.' " Over the years following her death, I have kept that saying and the faith which informed it tucked safely away in my memory for easy and frequent reference.

I also remember my final visit with my grandfather in the hospital. He had suffered another in a series of heart attacks. During our conversation we talked about a real variety of contemporary issues, funny stories and special memories. Toward the end of our conversation, he must have sensed what I feared was soon to happen. With a cheerful kindness in his voice and on his face, he assured me that he was ready to go home to heaven if the Lord was ready for him. He loved his Lord, his church, his family and friends. He had been faithful to the end. There was no fear or uncertainty about what was in store for him. Even with my faith firmly in place, there was a part of me that wanted to believe that grandparents did not die. They stayed around to tell embarrassing tales about your parents, feed you good food, and teach you wise and funny stories. So when my grandfather reminded me of his mortality and assured me of his faith in Jesus Christ and his acceptance of the gift of eternal life, it took some time for me to digest all of his food for thought.

In both of those cases I wanted my grandparents to stay around longer, but the time we did have together was truly blessed. Their lives had been long, fruitful and satisfying. Unfortunately, that scenario is not always played out when death invades our existence. A child stops breathing in the middle of the night to leave parents and friends asking, "Why?" A normally healthy member of the church is stricken by an illness and dies before anyone can truly realize what is happening.

5

The excitement and joy of Christmas is tempered with an unexpected death. An accident snatches away a productive, vital member of the community. A young couple grieve because their child never enjoyed that luxurious first gulp of air. Suicide, with all its savage mystery, stuns everyone in its path.

Pastors and laypeople alike have been close to some or all of those tragic situations. They are either looking for the right words to say or they yearn to hear the right words spoken to them. The funeral service presents a tremendous opportunity for healing, hope-filled words to be shared.

The 22 meditations in this volume have been researched, designed and delivered in situations quite similar to those I have already described. You will find new ideas on how to approach tough situations. An assortment of preaching styles will spark your own imagination as you work with your own grief ministry. Through it all you will be reminded of the power of God's word and his family to provide effective, caring ministry to the bereaved.

Michael L. Thompson
November, 1993

Business Leader
Isaiah 25:6-9; Romans 8:31-35, 37-39; John 5:24-29

1 — The Conclusion Of The Message

By Mark P. Zacher, Associate Pastor
Trinity Lutheran Church
Camp Hill, Pennsylvania

The funeral was held on June 18th and so the opening illustration was especially appropriate.

On June the 18th, 1915, 175 years ago to this day, the combined forces of Austria, Russia, Great Britain and Prussia, under the leadership of the British general Arthur Wellesly Wellington, engaged the powerful army of the French Empire, under Napoleon Bonaparte, near a Belgium town named Waterloo. By a pre-arranged agreement, the British army, at the end of that day, was to signal back to the coast the result of the outcome of that battle through a code of smoke signals. The message would then be communicated across the English Channel and hand-delivered to the King of England in the city of London.

On the evening of June 18th, at the conclusion of that fierce battle, in which more than 25,000 men lost their lives, the English communication experts on the coast awaited the smoke signal declaring either the victory or the defeat of their army. And, soon, their waiting came to an end.

Over the top of a distant hillside, they were able to make out the distinctive smoke signal message from Waterloo and they began to translate it. The first word was unmistakenly the code for "Wellington." The second, following soon after, was the signal for the word "defeated." When those two words were received, a sudden shift occurred in the wind and the sky quickly filled with dark, low clouds. Now it would be impossible to receive any more smoke signal messages. But it seemed that they had received all that they needed. Their message unmistakenly read: "Wellington defeated." And so, with great sorrow, they turned and they communicated that fact across the English Channel and the message was delivered to the King in London.

That night, all of England was heartbroken to receive the news that their general, Arthur Wellesly Wellington, and his forces had been defeated by the French emperor, Napoleon Bonaparte — for it now seemed as if there would be no way in which to stop the expansion of Napoleon's power.

That next morning, again the British agents on the coast searched the skies for more smoke signals from Waterloo and again they received a message. It began with the same word: "Wellington." The next word was also the same: "defeated." But this time, with a clear blue sky overhead, there came a third word. To complete the sentence came the code for the name "Napoleon." You see, the correct message, all along, had read: "Wellington defeated Napoleon." And, unfortunately, they had only been getting a part of the truth!

If I may suggest something to you on this date, 175 years later — I happen to think that often when we face the reality and the experience of death we may be something like those British agents along the coast of the English Channel. We may, unfortunately, only be getting a part of the message and a portion of the truth. But, let me tell you what I mean.

I imagine that when many people heard or read about the death of ＿＿＿＿＿＿ all that they thought about was that his life had come to an end. No longer would he be a respected business leader of our community. No longer would he be here for his business associates or for his employees or, most importantly, for his wife and his daughters and his son and his grandchildren and his great-grandchildren and his brothers and his sister and his friends. No, now he was gone and the message that seems to be communicated is that: "＿＿＿＿＿ has been defeated!" — defeated by his age and by his "miner's asthma" and by his pneumonia and by his cancer, defeated, in fact, by death itself.

You know though, as I think about it, perhaps it is not unusual for people to think in that way. I would even imagine, that that was the way many, many people thought way back in the city of Jerusalem on a Friday and a Saturday during the celebration of Passover. They had seen a man by the name of Jesus Christ die a cruel death on a cross on a hillside called Calvary and undoubtedly they thought that the message that was being communicated was that Jesus had been defeated. But, you know, as well as I do, that that is only a part of the story. You know, as well as I do, that following that Friday and that Saturday came a Sunday that has forever since been known of as Easter. And, you know, again as well as I do, that Jesus Christ burst forth from the tomb and put aside the chains of death. We know that the message of the cross is not completed until a final word is added. The message is not: "Jesus was defeated." No, rather the message is: "Jesus has defeated death!"

Well, I am here this day to tell you that that is also the conclusion of the message that we should see in the death of _____. The message of this day and of this hour is not that _____ has been defeated. No, the message rather is that _____, because of what our Lord Jesus Christ has done and given to him as a gift, has also defeated death.

_____, your husband and father and grandfather and brother and friend, has defeated death!

Paul, in our second lesson, told us that there is nothing that can separate us from God's love. Now that also includes death. You see, death cannot separate us from God, for death has been defeated. And, one day, we will all, every single one of us, learn the truth of that victory firsthand, as has _____.

No, this death is not the end. No, in a way, in fact, it is only the beginning — the beginning of eternal life and God's victory over death for _____ and for you and for me.

9

2 — Healed Once Again

By Anna M. Ritter, Pastor
Messiah Lutheran Church
Mifflintown, Pennsylvania

God heals.

That might sound like a contradiction of reality to us who are here, at this time, in this place, who are gathered to commend _____ to God, _____ whose illness struck so suddenly and who sickened and died so rapidly. But let me read you a gospel text, one well-known to us all. The evangelist Matthew tells us:

> _Getting into a boat, Jesus crossed over and came to his own city. And behold, they brought to him a paralytic, lying on his bed; and when Jesus saw their faith, he said to the paralytic, "Take heart, my son; your sins are forgiven." And behold, some of the scribes said to themselves, "This man is blaspheming." But Jesus, knowing their thoughts, said, "Why do you think evil in your hearts? For which is easier, to say, "Your sins are forgiven," or to say, "Rise, and walk?" But that you may know that the son of man has authority on earth to forgive sins," — and he then said to the paralytic — "Rise, take up your bed and go home." And he rose and went home. When the crowds saw it, they were afraid, and they glorified God, who had given such authority to men._

God does heal. And he does so in more than one way. He does heal physically. Every one of us has been healed physically by God, over and over. Sometimes, through the natural course of healing that God placed in the natural order of things: broken bones mend, colds run their course. Some of us have been healed through the wisdom God has imparted to medical science of our time; from pneumonia, heart attacks, premature births. Perhaps you or someone you know have even been healed in ways we still consider real miracles of healing by God, because we as yet do not know how they happen: remission from cancer, or awakening from a long-term coma. All these healings come from God. And we are all healed by God again and again by one of these, his methods. _____, too. Over and over during her life.

But the time is going to come for each one of us when God is simply not going to heal us in the physical way. Nothing in God's creation was created to last forever in this physical state: not stars, mountains, rivers, insects, birds, and not us. How often we forget that for all those people Jesus healed from illness during his ministry, that healing was not forever; it was a one-time healing, and all those people would get sick again sometime in the future. And even die sometime in the future, from something God deigned not to cure.

But in Matthew's gospel text, Jesus said something else besides "Rise and walk" to that sick man. He also said, "Your sins are forgiven."

Physical healing is not the only healing God provides. There is also spiritual healing, the forgiveness of sin. Physical healing of illness leads to continued life on this earth. Spiritual healing of sin leads to life in heaven. Physical healing is temporary, because we all will die eventually, no matter how often God heals us before that time. Spiritual healing is forever. In fact the word "salvation" means "to heal," from the same root word as the English word salve, a healing ointment. Salvation is eternal healing. And, it is the only healing that Christ died on the cross that we might have; therefore, it is the most important of all healings.

At the time of a funeral, we gather to celebrate God's healing. Obviously we are not celebrating the physical healing, for the final illness that brings us here is always the one that God has ordained not to heal. But rather we gather to celebrate God's healing us of the sickness of sin through Jesus Christ, our Lord. And _____'s Lord. The Lord of life. "For God so loved the world that he gave his only son, that whoever believes in him should not perish but have eternal life."

Some healing is better than other healing. _____ was healed many times by God in the natural course of her life, over and over, I'm sure; otherwise, she would not have been the strong, healthy woman she was up to a few months ago. But that was not her most important healing. Most importantly, her sins were forgiven by God, and the healing of salvation was hers. And that's the healing that counts now. As eventually it was the only healing that counted for all those whom Jesus cured in person during his ministry. And it is the only healing that will count for you and me in the end.

And so we thank God for his healing _____, as she joins all those whom God has healed before her. And we pray that through Jesus Christ we may join them in that eternal healing when our time comes. Thanks be to God!

3 — Hallowed Ground

By B. David Hostetter, Retired Pastor
Wolcott, New York

This is hallowed ground
Created from nothing
But the thought of God
Who became Creator
In the making of it.
This is a hallowed place
Made sacred by the Divine One,
Who called good
All living things
That move
In and on
Under and over
Through and around
This good earth.
This is hallowed ground
To which we return
The common elements
Made uncommon by love.
This is hallowed earth
For to it we return
The elemental remains
of _____.
This is holy ground
Now containing
What is no longer animated
By the breath of God.
This plot of ground
is hallowed by love:
Parental love —
The divine One
Who creating

Male and female
In the divine likeness
Became the first parent.
This plot is hallowed
by the married love
of _____ and _____
who fathered and mothered
begot and conceived
birthed and cared for children.
This plot of earth
Is hallowed by family love
Of children and grandchildren
In unbroken chain
Of human life,
Ancestral ties
To the one who parents us still.
This is holy ground
Made sacred
By the faith
of the church
of Jesus Christ
Who was no less than God
Born of Mary,
Taught by his parents,
Living for others,
Teaching us,
Praying for us,
Dying for us,
Rising from death before us
To that most holy place
Where he with _____
Waits for us.
This we sincerely believe
in the name of God,
who is fatherly, brotherly, motherly,
Our God, one God,
forever.
Amen.
(Pastor spreads a handful of earth as may others.)

Child
2 Samuel 12:16-23

4 — The Things Which Remain When All Is Lost

By Thomas A. Pilgrim, Senior Pastor
St. John United Methodist Church
Atlanta, Georgia

There is a story in the Old Testament book of 2 Samuel which I want to share with you. When King David and his wife Bathsheba had their first child it became apparent the boy would not live very long. For seven days the child lay near death.

During this time King David was in a period of mourning and fasting. He lay all night upon the ground asking God that the child might live.

Finally, on the seventh day the child died. The servants of King David were afraid to go in and tell the king what had happened. They were afraid he would do some harm to himself. But, when the king saw his servants whispering to each other he knew the child had died. He asked them if it were so and they answered yes.

King David got up, washed, anointed himself, changed his clothes. Then he went to the house of the Lord and worshiped him. He then went home and asked for food.

The servants wanted to know why this sudden change. He answered, "While the child was still alive I fasted and wept, for I said, 'Who knows whether the Lord will be gracious?' But, now he is dead; why should I fast? Can I bring him back? I shall go to him; but, he shall not return to me."

I think if we were to put his words into modern language we would hear him saying to us, "I have had my heart broken by this. But now that it is over there is nothing else I can do, and life goes on."

I know this has been a tragic ordeal for all of you. You have come through the most difficult experience you could ever have. But, we must remember this great truth we see in this story of David and Bathsheba — the truth that we weep in the midst of our sorrow, but then we recognize the fact that life goes on and we must go on living.

The secret to living is not what our experiences do to us, but what we do with them.

This experience which you are having will have one of two results for you. If you let it this will break you. If you choose you may take it, and let it make you.

James W. Moore, a United Methodist minister in Texas, wrote a book a few years ago called, *You Can Get Bitter Or Better*. That is always the choice.

You can take this experience and use it, and let it mold your life, make your life better than it would have ever been had you not passed this way.

I know this experience is a time of loss for you. But in the midst of this loss of a child, I also want to remind you that all is not lost.

For one thing life's enduring values are not lost. Paul wrote that, "Faith, hope, and love abide." Those things cannot be destroyed. They are the things which last.

Christian faith will hold you up when nothing else will. It will see you through. Christian hope will make you strong. It will sustain you. Christian love, your love for each other and God's love for you will comfort you. These three things abide. They will last forever.

Then second, the comfort you find in God's mercy is not lost. God will hold you up. He will be near you. He will never forsake you, not even in "the valley of the shadow of death."

Third, the care and concern of your family has not been lost. They are with you. We all share this with you. You can lean on these people here who care for you.

Finally, the life of this child has not been lost. The finest part of _____ lives on. Jesus said, "In my Father's house there are many rooms." There is a room there for all of us and especially for those of whom Jesus said, "Let the children come unto me, and forbid them not, for to such belongs the kingdom of Heaven."

There is a place there for _____.

When Dr. Charles Allen's wife died, one of his church members said to him, "I'm sorry you lost your wife." He replied, "I haven't lost her. I know where she is."

We can say that today. We know where _____ is now.

A wise old retired preacher told me once that he had a funeral for a child who died at the age of six. It was obviously a heart-breaking time for that family. They said, "We hope when we see her again she will not have changed any, and will still be just like she is now." He thought a minute and said, "Oh, you know you don't mean that. You would not want her to always be like she is now. The next time you see her she will be the person God designed her to become. She will be perfect in every way — in love, in knowledge, in hope."

And, I say to you, the next time you see _____ she will be perfect in every way.

5 — Mystery Of Death

By John A. Terry, Pastor
The Congregational Church of Hollis
Hollis, New Hampshire

Opening

May the grace and peace of God, who raised Jesus from the dead, be with us all.

We gather here, in the face of the preciousness of life and of the mystery of death. _____ and _____, with the death of your child something has changed irrevocably: anticipation has been thwarted, hope has been dashed, possibility has been ended, a corner has been turned.

_____ and _____ for you, too, anticipation of a new life in your home was thwarted, and the possibility of having a brother or sister was ended.

In all of this there has been crying and hurt, anger and frustration, times of being scared and of holding one another, times of shouting and sobbing.

In all of this we are reminded of the frailty of life, and the mystery of death. At the same time, we are reminded of the constancy and dependability of God and God's promises, remembering both the "otherness" as well as the intimacy of God. This is a time to listen to the wisdom of the men and women who have gone that way before, and who have said in the midst of their suffering: Here am I, send me.

Today, as we stand here together and commit this unfulfilled life back to God, as we listen, as we cling to one another for strength and sustenance, we also will turn our faces to a new place in which to go — a new Jerusalem which is ahead for us, even as Jesus turned his face toward Jerusalem.

In such a time, our hope is in the God who does not leave, who cannot be separated, who embraces us with the warmth of a mother and the protection of a father, who walks with us in the surety of a brother or a sister. Nothing can separate us, Paul says, from the love of God. Nothing. That is our faith. That is our hope. May God grant us all the courage, the wisdom and the strength so to know, and so to be.

(A prayer may be read here.)

Readings From The Scripture
Psalm 23
Psalm 121
Job 19:25-27
2 Corinthians 4:7-11
2 Corinthians 5:16
Matthew 4:3-10
Matthew 11:28-30
John 14:25-27

(A poem may be read here.)

Prayers
Gentle God, born an infant in Jesus Christ in the family of Joseph and Mary, we thank you for this family who grieves this day. You know of the hope and promise that they felt in the coming of this child, and the defeat and anguish which overcomes them in this loss. Remind them that even as Jesus embraced the little children, so you embrace those who cross the boundaries of our lives and, by your grace, know the peace of your eternal home.

Sustain _____ and _____, _____ and _____. Kindle anew the ashes of joy in them. Grant the peace and confidence of your promise that in all things, in life and in death, you are God, and you are with us, both in this life and in the life to come. Through Jesus Christ our Savior.

Commendation

Holy God, by your mighty power you gave us life, and in your love you have given us new life in Jesus Christ. We now entrust this child to your merciful care. We do this in the faith of Christ Jesus, who died and rose again to save us and is now alive and reigns with you and the Holy Spirit in glory for ever. Amen.

May the peace of God, which beyond all understanding, keep your hearts and minds, in the knowledge and love of God and of our Lord Jesus Christ. Amen.

Older Man
2 Corinthians 5:1, 6-10; John 14:1-6

6 — To The Father's House

By James McKarns, Pastor
St. Paul's Catholic Church
North Canton, Ohio

The first scripture reading we heard today was written by Paul and sent, in the form of a letter, to the people who lived in Corinth, Greece. Paul says our lives on this earth are similar to living in a tent.

The gospel was written later, by the apostle John. He describes life beyond this earth, as living in the Father's house — quoting the words of Jesus. I think these two brief readings give a graphic picture of how we human beings are to view life in its entirety.

Here, on this earth, we are the tent people. A tent is not built but pitched, because it is meant to be only temporary. In these tent-days of our lives we stay but a brief time and then journey on. We are called pilgrim people rather than settlers. If we conceive of earthly life as being anything other than temporary, we deceive ourselves.

The number of days allotted to the travelers of earth differs with each individual. For our brother _____, his days totalled _____ years. As we grieve and lament his passing, we realize his _____ years exceeded the average life span for men. Even if he could have lived for 87 years or more, his leaving would have been just as difficult to accept, for we are never ready to say goodbye to a dear person who is close to us. So we remember Paul's words that we are the tent-people and when we come upon the scene, in birth, we know before long we will be leaving.

21

The real spiritual dimension, which is the happy side of life, now comes with the gospel message. Here John says there is a kingdom where we can dwell securely forever. No more tent living. We have moved into the Father's house. He quotes the words of Jesus, stating in the Father's house "there are many dwelling places." The old translation was "many mansions," i.e. there is room for all. Jesus must have known this concept would not be easily grasped, so he adds if it were not true he would never have said it. Besides there being a place prepared for us, the Lord furthermore promises he will come, receive us and take us to our eternal dwelling place. At the time of a funeral, these eternal truths become more clearly focused in our minds. We can so easily be absorbed in the cares of this temporary, tent life existence that we forget about the promise of eternal life.

The author, Charles Kettering, said: "We should all be concerned about the future because we will have to spend the rest of our lives there." _____ was aware of and often talked about the next life. The hardships and trials he faced convinced him that here we have but a nebulous stability.

Not only is this brief but it is filled with inconsistencies and contradictions. So much happens around us over which we have no control. Thus the only choice we have is how we decide to accept it. There is an area, however, where we have complete control and that is our faith response and relationship to the One who promises us a place in the Father's house.

We offer our prayers for _____ today, mindful of the many times we prayed together in church. I also extend my love and understanding to his dear wife of _____ years.

The famous 20th century poet, T.S. Eliot, once wrote: "In the end is my beginning." That too is the teaching of our faith, as we reflect on the words of Jesus.

We commend our brother, _____, to God's eternal home. There may he find that everlasting peace and security which the Lord has promised to all of us.

7 — In His Redeemer's Arms

By Charles R. Turbin, Pastor
Trinity Lutheran Church
Cedarburg, Wisconsin

_____ and _____, friends and loved ones of _____, dear friends in Christ, grace to you and peace from God, our Father and from our Lord and Savior, Jesus the Christ. Amen.

"And Jesus took them in his arms." What a beautiful picture that is of the love our Lord has for his children. There is a hotel or more probably a rooming house I know of called The Redeemer's Arms. Huge white letters are mounted on the side of the building announcing its name. Those many times I have driven past there, I've always thought how terrific it might be to answer the question, "Where do you live?" by saying, "Oh, I live in The Redeemer's Arms."

But that is exactly where _____ lived those all too brief 12 years — in his Redeemer's arms. Born on _____, his doctors determined that his chances for survival were pretty small. But there was this glimmer of life there ... this spark that just wouldn't be quenched. Just four days later, on _____, at _____, _____ was baptized, taken up and enfolded into those warm and loving arms of his Savior, Jesus Christ. And he would live the rest of his life there, in his Redeemer's arms.

_____ would still know the pain of tubes and tests and too many operations, but he also found comfort in knowing that during those difficult times, Jesus would watch over him.

He knew the frustration of not being able to do all the things that some of the other kids could do, but at the same time, he became an avid _____ fan, got into dinosaurs, enjoyed fishing with Grandpa _____, was a friendly adversary with his dog, _____, and looked forward, someday, to being a truck driver. He once asked Grandma _____ if she thought Jesus would have a semi in heaven for him to drive.

_____ found fun living in those loving arms, but mostly, the greatest blessing he received from Jesus was his faith. He had that strong child-like faith that our Lord would want all of us to have. In Matthew 18, Jesus says, "Truly I say to you, unless you turn and become like children, you will not enter the kingdom of heaven." Sunday school and worship were important to him, especially Easter Sunday worship. And he really enjoyed reading his Bible. _____ truly lived in his Redeemer's arms.

On _____, those arms peacefully and quietly took him from this life to the next. As God's baptized child, _____ died in the very same arms in which he had lived. In the face of that tragedy — the death of a child has frequently been called the ultimate tragedy — perhaps that is the greatest comfort we can have ... that _____ died in the arms of his Savior.

A poet writes:

> "I'll lend you for a little time a child of mine," God said,
> "For you to love the while he lives, and to mourn for
>   when he's dead ...
> It may be six or seven years, or twenty-two or three,
> But will you, 'till I call him back, take care of him
>   for me?"
> "We'll shelter him with tenderness, we'll love him while
>   we may,
> For all the happiness we've known, forever grateful
>   stay.
> But shall the angels call for him much sooner than we've
>   planned,
> We'll brave the bitter grief that comes, and try to
>   understand."

24

It is much sooner than you've planned, and that time to grieve has come. _____ will be missed. There is a void in your lives, _____ and _____, and in your hearts and home, there is an unoccupied place in Sunday school, the youth choir, and among his classmates that may never be filled._____ has died, and we are very sad. But at the same time, there is comfort in knowing that he died in the arms of his Lord. As Paul wrote, "For I am sure that neither life nor death, nor anything else in all creation will be able to separate us from the love of God in Christ Jesus, our Lord."

Finally, as Christians, there is one more assurance to which we need to cling, and that is this, that while there is strength and comfort in the tender arms of Christ, we were given hope when those very arms were stretched upon a cross. We who are left behind can live in that hope, because those outstretched arms are God's assurance that our sins have been forgiven — your sins, and my sins, and yes, _____ sins, too. The sacrifice that God required has been made on our behalf by his very Son. Jesus Christ was like us — he was us — and he died for us, in order that all of our sins might be forgiven. And they are.

But our hope can't quit there. Good Friday without Easter is just another tragedy. No, _____ faith was not only in the God of the cross, but also in the God of the resurrection, and it is his faith and ours, in that one and the same God, that even allow us to be here tonight. We have come to worship him.

Faith in the risen Christ is the very beginning of a new life. Christ is in the now ... he is able to touch us and give us blessings and peace now. And yet, his presence tonight is only the beginning of the victory and the resurrection God has in store for all his children.

That's the Easter promise. Oh, none of us can fully understand it, I suppose. And we really don't know all that lies ahead; but this we do know, that God has prepared a place for us, just as he did for his Son, Jesus, and for his son,

_____, as Paul writes in Romans 6:5, "For if we have been united with him in a death like his, we shall certainly be united with him in a resurrection like his." That is the promise into which we baptize ... that is the hope in which we live, and in which we die.

"And he took them in his arms and blessed them." _____ lived and died and lives eternally in the arms of Jesus. And there is hope and comfort for all of us in those warm and loving and outstretched arms, as well. God bless you and your good memories of _____.

Amen.

Suicide During Lent
Jeremiah 29:11-12; Romans 8:22-39; John 14:1-3, 18

8 — There Is No Condemnation

By Deborah D. Steed, Associate Pastor
Prince of Peace Lutheran Church
Loveland, Ohio

On behalf of the _____ family, I want to thank you for being here today to remember _____ and give thanks to God for his life. Death draws us together within a web of common, sometimes conflicting, feelings. Your presence and support are vital to this family and will be for some time to come.

Let us pray: Gracious God, gather us together under the banner of your Word. Pierce our darkness with your light. In the name of Christ our Lord. Amen.

Yesterday, after the 11 a.m. service here at _____, one of our senior members said to me, "My heart is broken." Of course her heart was broken. She had lost a member of her church family. She spoke for all of us then, and I daresay she speaks for all of us now.

_____: Our hearts are broken, too. We, too, have lost a member of our church family, a fellow committeeman, a brother in the choir, a co-worker, an employee, a boss, a friend, a neighbor. Because _____ is gone, something in us is gone.

And our hearts are broken for you. How many times have you heard, in these past four days, the words, "If I can do anything, please let me know?" There is much we can do, but there is much more that we cannot do, and that grieves us all.

As we rummage around in our sadness to find some comfort, the first place we turn is to our memories of _____ himself. We remember him as a man who loved his wife and daughters dearly, who was patient and gave you space when you needed it. He thought _____ and _____ were the cleverest two kids he'd ever seen. And he followed _____ short life with intense concern both for his grandson and for his daughter and son-in-law.

We also remember his love of music. How could we forget? He started singing in church choirs when he was a boy and carried it through in every church he joined. He infected the family with musical talent by passing on his gifts to the girls and making singalongs a special activity around the piano. Nothing pleased him more than for his daughters to play or sing on Sunday morning or perform in school productions.

_____ loved the church for more than its music. It was a center of his life, and he made it a center of the family's life. He brought to us a definite _____ slant on things. He jumped into committee work and long-range planning with the enthusiasm of a life-long member, even though he'd only been with us a short time. At every congregational dinner, he was a fixture in the kitchen, helping to prepare and clean up, because that's just what you do.

Each of you has some memory of _____, or perhaps of knowing him through _____. How good it is to have those dear memories of him. But memories alone will get us only so far. Then they drive us back to troubled waters. We need something more to help us through our pain today. We need the gospel word. And that word tells us some very important things.

First, it tells us that though our nagging questions may never be answered, we are not left alone with them. All of us are shaken. We wonder, "How could this happen?" "Why didn't I see the clues?" "What could I have said and done to prevent this?" "How can someone so close to me have been such a mystery?" Questions like this haunt us because we are so sorrowful and because we feel so powerless.

Some people believe that Christianity is primarily a religion of answers. But our faith is more profoundly a religion of presence. Even when the questions seem to have no answers, God is present for us in our confusion, guilt, and impotence. "We do not know how to pray as we ought, but the Spirit intercedes with sighs too deep for words." When we are grieving, answers comfort us far less than do the sighs of a fellow-traveller. God is that fellow-traveller.

Secondly, the word reminds us, in case we would ever forget, that God's love is unconditional. I believe that _____ knew that God forgave and accepted him even in those dark moments when he could not forgive or accept himself. Scriptures are clear on this: There is no condemnation for those who are in Christ Jesus. Not even our despair can change God's love, for it is steadfast. What is most important is not our feelings about ourselves, which go up and down, but God's acceptance of us which never wavers.

Thirdly, God himself has suffered, and, as the martyr Dietrich Bonhoeffer said, "Only a suffering God can help." How could our Lord possibly be put off by the feelings that constitute our grief, since those feelings are God's gift to us? Even though they can be strong and unwelcome, feelings are the vehicle for helping us travel through this time. God honors human emotion and stands by us in it, because God knows what it is like to have a part of yourself torn away by death.

This suffering God can also encourage us to be more aware of and accepting of our own brokenness. We live in a culture which sets unusually high standards of success and marks failure as the deadliest sin. And yet the very symbol of our faith, the cross, was at one time the ultimate sign of failure. Jesus of Nazareth was condemned as a charlatan, a fake. He was considered too much trouble to tolerate.

Why, then, do we find ourselves so unacceptable when we do not meet those cultural standards? If the cross teaches us anything, it is that because God accepts our brokenness, we must, too. God doesn't ask for perfection but for authenticity. Surely _____ death can push us to pray for the courage to look deeply inside ourselves and accept whatever we find there, as we know our Lord does. And we must remember that self-acceptance is a shining witness to God's acceptance. We know today, more than ever, how much the world needs to hear that good news.

Finally, this suffering God of ours can teach us how to live in community. We cannot afford to live for ourselves alone. We are indeed our brothers' and sisters' keepers, just as surely as they are ours. The church is designed to be a place where we are little Christs to one another. Because we are limited, sinful people, we need one another. When life is too dark for me, you can carry the candle of hope. When the burden is too heavy for you, I can share the load. When you are too despairing to pray, we can lift up our united voices on your behalf. Jesus never intended us to be anything except interdependent. Interdependence makes us less afraid to let others in to the secret places where we hurt, so that healing can begin.

This is the season of Lent. It is a natural time to dig more deeply into our spiritual center, to probe the critical questions of life. But it is also a time to look forward. For at the end of this season comes Easter. _____ knew about the resurrection. He knew about a Lord who can make the dead to rise to life eternal, wiping away all tears and bringing joy in the morning. We look to that morning, to that resurrection life which is ours even now, even in this hurtful, sorrowful time. Our risen Lord calls again to each of us from that Easter morning which is never lost in time, but comes to us again and again to raise us up. Amen.

9 — The March Of Death

By Merlin L. Conrad, Senior Minister
Calvary Reformed Church
Reading, Pennsylvania

When I was in seminary there was a picture hanging in our library that I will never forget. I have long since forgotten who the artist might have been, but the message was indelible. It was titled "The March of Death" and pictured death marching through the throngs of humanity calling, at will, whom he chose. He called the young and the old, the rich and the poor, the well and the infirmed. There was something else in that picture I remember and that is that there were those kneeling by the roadside, pleading to join his march, who were passed by. It seems to me that the message is clear that although death is indiscriminate, death finally does come to us all.

However, it makes a difference under what circumstances death calls us as to how we react. If death comes to a very young child, we react in anger; we are even so bold as to question how a good God could allow this to happen. If death comes to one in the prime of their life, our reaction is one of shock and alarm, but inevitably someone will be heard to say, "When it is my turn, that's the way I want to go, while I am active, with my boots on." If death comes as a result of a catastrophe — fire, earthquake, flood — although we are sympathetic, our reaction is one of frustration, for what could we have done to prevent it?

But this is not the way death has come this time. The way death has visited us now causes us to, at least, mingle our sorrow with the reaction of thanksgiving. Thanksgiving for the life we knew her to have had; thanksgiving that for her the

31

day of pain is over; thanksgiving that God, in his mercy, allowed a peaceful end.

But our thanksgiving does not veil our mourning, for indeed the rending of our hearts at the loss of love and memory is as old as humanity itself.

Some years ago there were two English explorers who discovered the sarcophagus of a little girl, estimated to be 4,000 years old. When they translated the hieroglyphics on the lid it read:

> *O my life, my love, my little one; if God had willed, I would have died for thee!*

So mourning is indeed ancient and our search for relief is equally ancient. Those of New Testament times are no exception. Paul, in writing to the Philippians, says that "Death is the desire to depart and to be with Christ." Taken in and of itself, there is comfort in that passage, but when we understand that to which Paul may have been referring, it brings us even more solace.

For you see, in Paul's day, the word depart literally meant to "break camp," and he must have been making reference to those nomadic people who surrounded every city's gate; who, at the command of the head of the tribe, would break camp and move to a place better for them. Now the people in those tents were not dead. The tent was simply collapsed so that they might move on. So it is in the life of a Christian, when the tent in which we are living is collapsed. We, too, are then free to move to our eternal home, a place better for us.

Having said all of this, may I confess to you as well that at the final analysis it is a very difficult task for a pastor to try to fashion into words the meaning of the life that we here honor. So, if you will forgive my being personal, may I share with you, not my words, but the words of my father, who along with _____, shared the same generation, the same dedication to hard work and simplicity, the same love of music and God's creation.

32

It happened this way. Shortly before his death, he was asked by his home pastor to write a daily devotion during Lent to be shared with the rest of the parish. In that writing he told of a day that spring, when he was in our basement sprouting potatoes, getting ready for spring planting. And he said, as he looked at those potatoes in the box, they were old, they were wrinkled, and in some cases they were moldy. And for those who would know no better, they would conclude the potatoes were useless and should be thrown away; but he saw in them a sprig, a sprout, that when planted, would come to life again.

Then he said something very interesting. He said: "Some day soon people will look at me in a box and I'll be old, and I'll be wrinkled, and for those who know no better they will say, 'He is dead.' But don't you believe it, for there is a sprig and a sprout, that when planted, will come to life again."

The Lord gave and now the Lord has taken away. Let us thank God that, when we are part of death's procession, he steps forward and takes us into his procession of life.

Congregation Experiencing Several
Deaths In A Brief Period
Psalm 46

10 — When The Boat Keeps Rocking

By Robert A. Noblett, Senior Minister
Congregational Church
Kalamazoo, Michigan

On a fourth of July weekend when I was a fairly young man, a friend of my father's invited a friend of mine and me to go on a boat ride with him on Conesus Lake, one of the so-called Finger Lakes in central New York state. Even as a young man I recognized this person to be one who trafficked with what is dicey, but for some reason we capitulated to pressure and got into the boat. To make short a long story, it was a frightening experience. The man drove at excessive speeds and the boat never did stop rocking. And because it never did, neither did I until I was once more on terra firma. And I'm sure I shook for a while after that.

As a congregation we are feeling these days that our congregational boat keeps rocking. And it has been! Since January we have lost through death eight church members and many of them were extremely active in the life of our congregation. We will be reminded of their absence for a long time.

This rockiness has been expressed in a question that many have been rhetorically asking: When is this going to stop? Believe me, if it were in my pastoral purview I would be glad to issue an edict that declared — no more deaths until a later time! But it isn't and so we talk today about what we do when the boat keeps rocking.

We can remind ourselves that more than we realize the boat is always rocking, but in recent days it has been rocking more than usual. When we think about congregational life, change is far more norm than aberration. Every little while someone is changing jobs, a child is born, an illness occurs, a family crisis develops and is processed, a family or individual moves out of the area or a new person or family becomes involved in the life of the congregation. This process of change is even more accentuated in a university town, what with the constant movement in and out of students, faculty and staff. Even on a lake that seems as smooth as glass the boat moves ever so slightly.

When the boat rocks we can also be there for each other. We have been doing just that in recent days. Many have commented on the number of changes that have been occurring and in the process of hearing those kinds of questions and responding to them we are there for each other.

Years back I enjoyed an amusement park ride that operated on the basis of centrifugal force. The ride was a huge cylinder and people filled up spaces along the edge of a huge circle. When all were in place, this cylinder began to rotate faster and faster until the floor on which people were standing gave way and all were pinned against the rotating wall. It was fun — for a while — but then it felt good to have the floor returned under one's feet.

When the boat won't stop rocking, we help each other regain our footing by the age-old process of mutuality in friendship. It is a simple mutuality, but indeed so simple that we often fail to honor it. We might call this mutuality a mutuality of availability. First, I will be available to you. I will clear my mind, create a space for you within myself, and invite you to confidently share your thoughts, feelings and impressions with me. And I will do my best to listen to you in a non-judgmental, loving and caring way. Secondly, this mutuality of availability means that there will come moments when you will do for me what I have done for you. You will clear your mind and heart, create for me an inner space, and allow me to share my thoughts, feelings and impressions with you and have them similarly received. A very simple mutuality, but one that is violated with great regularity.

Think about it. On the one hand, can you not call to mind someone who in their bearing toward you wants you to do all the listening while they do all the talking? Then when you go to talk, their ears are not available. Or on the other hand, do we not know people who will never disclose themselves and want only to be someone with whom others share the contents of their hearts?

The simplest illustration of what we are talking about is something we have in our hand hundreds and hundreds of times a year. Telephones have receiving components and sending components. Who ever heard of a telephone where you could only listen and not speak, or speak and not listen? In Christian friendships we do both and that mutuality is wonderfully beneficial when the boat won't stop rocking.

Third, when the boat keeps rocking we can pray. We can use a prayer that has been in the household of faith for years or we can speak with God as we feel led. We can pray in our homes or autos, or we can come to the sanctuary, if that facilitates our hunger to be connected to God. Our prayers can be audible or our thoughts sent God-ward can be the expression of our praying. Maybe we tend to be too mechanical about prayer. In fact, I think it is a much more natural act than we have made it out to be. My guess is that our praying tends to be far more circular than it should be; better to pray spontaneously and freshly, hungering to be connected to the will of God. George Macdonald got right to the point when he wrote, " 'O God!' I cried and that was all. But what are the prayers of the whole universe more than expansion of that one cry? It is not what God can give us, but God we want." Matthew Fox in our day has said much the same thing: "It is almost as if to pray is, after Jewish and Jesus' teaching, to stand daily before mystery and before the Giver of Life even in one's most insignificant actions."

If prayer has become rote for us, we need to let its mystery claim us afresh. We don't need to analyze it; we need to embrace it, to sit comfortably with its perplexities and allow its hopes to nourish us.

A recent scientific study reported in the *Journal of the American Medical Association* found that hospitalized heart patients had fewer complications when other people prayed for their recovery. Two groups, each numbering about 200 patients, were studied. Several Christians prayed for persons in the experimental group. Patients in the control group did not receive prayers. Neither group was told whether or not they were prayed for.

There is a mystery about it all. And I am asking that we trust the mystery.

When the boat won't stop rocking, prayer can help us.

The boat always rocks, sometimes harder than others. When we feel that rocking we can seek out our sisters and brothers in Christ and we can pray.

And all this leads us to a rediscovery of the fact that when the earth changes and the mountains shake and the waters roar and the mountains tremble, the bedrock of our security is God. When we say goodbye to our children as they make their way into adulthood, God ultimately is the bedrock of our security, as God is when we stand at the edge of a grave and say our farewells, as we consider our own mortality and as we rock and reel under the force of anything in life that shakes us to the foundations.

Hence the psalmist's simple and yet utterly truthful declaration: "God is our refuge and strength, a very present help in trouble. Therefore we will not fear ..."

And the psalmist continues: "There is a river whose streams make glad the city of God, the holy habitation of the Most High." Ever wonder about that river and what it means? I did for years. The poetry is beautiful but it is even more beautiful when we realize the psalmist is talking about the life-giving fountain of God's presence.

The psalm ends: "The Lord of hosts is with us; the God of Jacob is our refuge." And the good news for this Sabbath or for any day when the rocking of the boat bothers us is declared when we add one word to the psalm — "The Lord of hosts is with us; the God of Jacob is our refuge." — still.

11 — Playing In The Streets

By James W. Weis, Pastor
Christ Lutheran Church
Shrewsbury, Pennsylvania

Thus says the Lord: "I will return to Zion, and will dwell in the midst of Jerusalem; Jerusalem shall be called the faithful city, and the mountain of the Lord of hosts shall be called the faithful mountain." Thus says the Lord of hosts: "Old men and old women shall again sit in the streets of Jerusalem, each with staff in hand because of their great age. And the streets of the city shall be full of boys and girls playing in the streets."

People were bringing little children to [Jesus] in order that he might touch them; and the disciples spoke sternly to them. But when Jesus saw this, he was indignant and said to them, "Let the little children come to me; do not stop them; for it is to such as these that the kingdom of God belongs. Truly I tell you, whoever does not receive the kingdom of God as a little child will never enter it." And he took them up in his arms, laid his hands on them, and blessed them.

Zechariah's world was a terrible and scary place to be. The prophet had returned, with a few others, from exile in Babylon. But the Jerusalem to which he returned was very different from the Jerusalem he had left. Her walls were broken down, her houses vacant and destroyed, the glorious temple in rubble.

But worst of all was the loneliness and isolation. Jerusalem was no longer a friendly place to be. Most of her people were gone, scattered God knows where, perhaps to the ends of the earth. The streets of the city, once filled with vendors and shoppers, with people sitting and talking, with boys and girls playing, were silent, eerie, and deserted. Indeed, it appeared as though God himself had abandoned his city. A terrible place to be! An awful situation to be in!

Further, Zechariah's Jerusalem was haunted by ghosts! Ghosts that plagued people by day. Ghosts that came to them in the darkness of the night, and whispered in their ears, and kept them from sleep. "God has forsaken you. You have brought this sadness upon yourselves. There is no way out. You are doomed to live in your loneliness forever. You are trapped in our own past!"

So the ghosts spoke. And the people, try as they may, could not escape the ghosts and their terrifying voices. A terrible situation indeed!

But God always has the last Word, and he spoke that Word through the mouth of Zechariah. Yes, the people of Jerusalem were facing many difficulties — loneliness and desolation, hunger and poverty, sickness and death. And, yes, these things were the result of the people's sin. But God was bringing a new order of things! The Lord said: "I will return to Zion, and will dwell in the midst of Jerusalem." And the loneliness and isolation will be gone: "Old men and old women shall again sit in the streets of Jerusalem . . . And the . . . city shall be full of boys and girls playing in its streets."

I think these words speak to us today. We have come here in great sadness. Death has broken into our lives. A child, _____, has been born dead, and that makes us feel pain and sorrow. Like the exiles of old, we too are in a dreadful place.

And we too face the ghosts. Did we do something wrong? Is there some way we could have prevented all this? Why did this happen to us? Has God abandoned us? Is he punishing us? We carry the ghosts around with us each day. And they come to us when we lie on our beds, and sleep escapes us. They whisper the most dread accusations in our ears. They trouble us, and they try to entrap us in our past.

But we too can look to the future! The future is God's kingdom — a place where he is with us, and where there is no sin or death, and where our children are not taken away from us. In this kingdom there are no ghosts, but only hope.

This kingdom began when Jesus, who himself came as a little child, came into this world of sin and death. And, even in the midst of our sadness and isolation, we can enter this kingdom because of the One who came to drive off the ghosts of our past. In spite of our past, Jesus loves us, and he loves all children, and he bids us become like children, and come to him and depend on him for everything.

And so, because of this King, the words of Zechariah take on a new meaning. They dispel our ghosts, and they call us to a future in God's new Jerusalem. And in that holy city, there shall be no more sorrow, or sighing, or pain. For the problems that plague this world have all been destroyed in the activity of God on the cross. And in this kingdom, where all is perfect joy, unstained by isolation and tragedy, we shall be with our children. Like Zechariah of old said, we shall sit in safety in the streets of this new Jerusalem, and "the ... city shall be full of boys and girls playing in the streets." And _____, healthy and strong, shall be there too!

12 — In Stride

By Ruth L. Boling, Associate Pastor
Bedford Presbyterian Church
Bedford, New Hampshire

We have come today to celebrate the life of _____;
beloved son, grandson, brother, and friend. We have come
to offer our thanks to God for giving him to us — even for
so short a time as _____ years — and we have come to commend him now to God's eternal keeping as it has been promised
to us in the holy scriptures.

After a long and quietly courageous battle with Hodgkin's
Disease, of this we can be certain, that for _____ there
is now no more pain, no more fear, no sorrow. Although our
knowledge of eternal matters is limited, of this much we can
be certain — that he is with God, that he is wrapped in the
loving arms of God his maker.

For "whether we live or whether we die, we are the Lord's,"
say the scriptures. So, "let not your hearts be troubled, neither
let them be afraid." For Jesus said, "In my Father's house
there are many rooms. If it were not so would I have told you
that I go to prepare a place for you?" Let us thank God for
these promises!

And let us thank God for _____. What a great guy.
I only had the privilege of knowing _____ through the
last few months of his illness. Most of you knew him far better than I. But during that time and during the past few days
I've learned, I've heard stories, I've seen collages of pictures:
_____ with _____, _____ growing up,
_____ with his friends, his car, _____ . . ."

41

Let us thank God for _____, who said things like, "you know you have a good car stereo if your rearview mirror shakes." And "I'll always have time for you, Dad."

_____, whose mother heard him say, only once, throughout his long illness, "Why me?" Only once. _____, who had a way with children, and animals, and babies — never losing his gentle touch even in the hospital . . . _____, the kid on the skateboard, taking apart bikes and televisions, the "_____," until he "retired," listening to music, wearing concert t-shirts, creating computer graphics with _____. You who knew _____ remember him in countless specific ways, with his own particularities and very human traits.

Let us thank God for this child, this young man, who touched so many people in his unassuming way, who never complained, who always answered "fine" or "okay" when asked how he was doing. Whether it was his doctors and nurses, his friends, his pastors, the _____, his sister, his grandmothers or his own parents, none who visited _____ in the hospital were unmoved by his courage.

"He is the bravest person I ever knew," said one who loved him very much.

Your love for _____ may cause you to feel angry that he is gone. It may cause you to ask the question "Why?" Why him? Why so young? Why such a great guy as him? Why not some other jerk instead?

It is human and natural to ask these questions. But in your asking remember this, that _____ own mother only heard him ask that question once. Only once did he ask "why me?" So ask, but do not dwell on these questions. For they are unanswerable. We don't and we will never know why, _____. It's not for us to know.

Instead the Bible helps us to know these things: that even though we walk through the valley of the shadow of death we need fear no evil for God is with us, his rod and staff comfort us and that nothing can ever separate us from the love of Christ. Neither death nor life, nor angels nor principalities, nor things present nor things to come, nor powers, nor height nor depth, nor cancer, nor anything else in all creation will be able to separate us from the love of God in Christ Jesus our Lord.

In the last Old Testament passage that was read today from Isaiah 65, it talked about "the new Jerusalem" saying "no more shall there be an infant that lives but a few days ..." The "new Jerusalem" is a metaphor for the life beyond life that God promises to us. "Like the days of a tree shall the days of my people be," God goes on to say. In other words, no one will be cut off early in the new Jerusalem. No more shall there be an infant that lives but a few days, or a teenager that lives but a few years. Our days with God shall be like the days of a tree. (Not like the too-short blooming of the cut daffodil shall our days be, but like the days of a tree!)

I know that this is an excruciating loss for many of you. Do reach out to each other in your grief. Strengthen and support each other. Go to your pastor, or a counselor, or a trusted friend. Cry.

And carry on. Stay in stride with the rest of your lives. In thanksgiving to God for the life of _____, stay in stride. Amen.

Murder Victim
Job 19:23, 27a; Matthew 27:45-50

13 — Answers To Consider

By James W. Addy, Pastor
St. John's Lutheran Church
Clinton, South Carolina

This meditation was preached at the funeral of a 60-year-old woman who was shot to death by her son in their home. The woman's husband was resting in another room of the home when the shooting took place. The son remained at the scene until the police arrived.

We all know that a day will come when family and friends will gather to conduct funeral services for each of you. So, in that broad sense, we knew that this day would come for _____. We knew that _____ would die someday. She faced death by warding off a form of cancer. More recently she confronted the dangers of a stroke. Had any one of a number of health concerns caused her death, we would be gathered as we are to mourn her loss, to cherish fond memories of her, to share our grief, to lament her death. The violent nature of her death has heightened our emotions, and given us new ones. Bewilderment, anger, shame, regret, all add to the jumble of our emotions. And at times, disbelief, numbness, and shock take over in order to protect us. In these circumstances, our sorrow, our mourning, seem all the more compound.

At most deaths we wonder why. A death like this one causes us to ask why even more strongly, more searchingly. Why? Why did this happen? Was it hallucination? Was it mental illness? Was it a chemically induced destruction of the power of reason? Was it a love/hate emotion suddenly tilted out of balance? Was it the power of evil and sin? Was it some incomprehensible part of a plan the purpose of which may never be understood? The question, why?, taunts us. It will for years to come.

We are in the depths of pain and sorrow. The question of why only throws us deeper into despair and depression. Therefore, I propose that the why question is not ours to ask today. There are other truly more important questions before us today. They come in many forms and meanings. Some of you may be asking, "What does this do to the rest of my life?" Others may be asking, "How can I overcome this?" Others, "What good can come of this?" Still others may wonder, "How can this be avoided?" Some of you will have questions I can't even imagine.

Even though I do not assume to know the questions most urgent to you at this time, I shall be so bold as to propose answers to your questions in light of the situation. You may formulate your own questions as we explore answers that speak to us in the depths of sorrow.

You, _____ family, husband, children, sister, brother, and all relatives — also close friends and neighbors — are in the depths of sorrow. You will grieve over _____ death and the manner in which it occurred. You are not alone. We share your sorrow. We are all brought together today into the depths of sorrow and loss. In this situation, regardless of what our pressing question is, the psalmist and other scripture writers have a message, answers, for us to consider.

One psalmist wrote: "Out of the depths I cry to thee, O Lord! Lord, hear my voice." Out of our depths, O Lord, we cry to you. Lord, hear our voices. If you, O Lord, mark iniquities, who can stand? Yet there is forgiveness with you. Hope, therefore, is the Lord! For with the Lord there is steadfast love, and with him is plenteous redemption.

The psalmist wrote in a time of despair and sorrow. He wrote in a time when the people were in the depths. Out of the depths he called desperately to the Lord. Out of the depths he knew a Lord who offered forgiveness, hope, steadfast love, and plenteous redemption. He offers us an answer to our troubling questions.

When we think of being in the depths, no other biblical person comes to mind more appropriately than Job. Job lost all he had, wealth, sons and daughters, and great herds. He was even plagued with sores. Out of the depths of his despair and sorrow he had plenty of questions. He wanted to know who and what for? He questioned God; he struggled with God. But he never gave up on God. For in all his misery, Job could still say, "I know that my Redeemer lives, and at the last . . . I shall see God." Maybe our questions have to do with redemption. Out of our depths we can know that our redeemer lives. He who can give us new life lives; we can see him!

In another psalm, a psalmist writes, "God is our refuge and strength, a very present help in trouble." Though the earth changes and the mountains fall into the sea, we shall not fear. The God of Jacob is our refuge. When we find ourselves in such depths of sorrow and bewilderment as now, God is our refuge and strength. He is our very present help. Trouble has overwhelmed us. Yet, we are not abandoned. God is with us. We turn to him for strength and comfort. If our questions deal with finding strength to go on, the psalmist offers an answer. Out of our depths, God is our refuge.

It may have seemed very odd to have read a part of the crucifixion story at a funeral service. But when we consider being in the depths of pain and sorrow, we may sometimes falsely assume that God doesn't understand what we are experiencing. Jesus himself cried to God out of the depths of suffering and sorrow. If our questions deal with forsakenness; it will help us to know that the one who saves us, God's very son, felt forsaken as well. Most Bible scholars and interpreters believe Jesus was quoting the 22nd Psalm. It is a psalm that begins in anguish with a sense of forsakenness but ends with confidence in God. It proclaims that God will not hide his face from the afflicted. The Easter stories assure us that Jesus

46

was not forsaken. God was with him through his suffering, and raised him to live and rule eternally as Lord and Savior of us all. Out of our depths we may feel forsaken — but we are not! If in our pain we should question whether God is with us or not, or even if he cares, let us remember the cross of Christ. The Lord does not hide his face from our affliction.

The apostle Paul sums it up for us. "It is Christ Jesus, who died, yes, who was raised from the dead, who is at the right hand of God, who indeed intercedes for us? Who shall separate us from the love of Christ?" To which he proclaims: "Nothing!" Nothing shall separate us from the love of Christ. Not tribulation, not family tragedy, not distress, not things present, not things to come, not life, not death. Nothing in all creation will be able to separate us from the love of God in Christ Jesus our Lord. If we should wonder about the love of God, Paul offers us an answer. God's love in Christ Jesus is an enduring love, a steadfast love, a redeeming love. Nothing shall separate us from his love.

Out of the depths of our sorrow; out of our jumbled emotions, we cry to the Lord. Lord, hear our voices. We mourn the loss of _____ and the turmoil brought to the family. We remember with thankfulness the qualities of _____ which endeared her to us. Let us move beyond the immediate question of why, to see that God offers us answers to many other pressing questions. Out of our depths we cry to the Lord. He hears our voices and offers us: forgiveness and redemption; hope and steadfast love; refuge and strength; his very presence with us; comfort and understanding; and the assurance that nothing, nothing in all creation, separates us from his love in Jesus Christ our Lord. Amen.

47

Christmas Eve Suicide
Luke 2:10-11

14 — Good News At A Bad Time!

By Richard E. Merrick, Pastor
North Port Community UCC
North Port, Florida

A tragedy has come into our lives! We are stunned and distracted, but we must not despair; by the grace of God, we do not have to be afraid. The greater the sorrow, so much greater the power of God to give us the faith that makes us more than conquerors. This faith helps us to look up and hope. This faith enables us to hear the good news of the angel again this special day: "Do not be afraid ... to you is born ... a Savior ..." Christians need not feel that they are left without comfort at a time such as this. God has sent Jesus the Christ to be our Savior, to do something for us that we are unable to do for ourselves, to bring us to a right relationship with the Eternal One, God!

In this uncertain life, death may suddenly crash into our presence without notice, and we stand, unable to speak before the unsearchable wisdom of God. When the mind is troubled, normal thought processes and sound judgment are suspended. All sense of responsibility is lost. The only explanation for this tragedy is to be found in an illness that confuses the thinking process and brings on depressive moods. In all love and concern we want to believe today that because of such an illness, all sense of values was lost and there was no longer a responsibility for those actions taken on the part of our departed sister in the faith. We must leave the entire matter in the hands of a loving God and know that our gracious Creator understands us better than we do ourselves. God is merciful and full of compassion. Each of the Lord's children in distress is made acceptable through the Savior, Jesus Christ.

Some of the sting can then be taken out of this tragic hour. We are troubled and sorrowful, but not despairing. We can and do receive comfort from the Word of God: "Do not be afraid ... to you is born ... a Savior ..." We believe that all things, even the tragedies of this life, are in the hands of our merciful God. Even though many times things happen to us which are earthshaking, one thing cannot happen to us — we shall not be left alone! This is the promise of Christ to us; we shall perish but have eternal life.

We are living in troublesome times of national and international upheaval, of wars and rumors of wars, of false prophets and deceivers who lead people in strange paths. If ever there was a time for Christians to hear the Word of God, to reaffirm their faith in Jesus the Christ, to stand firmly together in unity of spirit, that time is now.

This Jesus, the Savior who has redeemed us, gives us a peace which passes all understanding. No matter what we must face in this life, God reconciles us through Christ, and we can face life with renewed courage, knowing that the Savior has been born for us.

May God, in abundant mercy, comfort us and in time heal the deep wounds which this tragedy has caused in our lives. We believe that God knows best. We place our future in God's hands, whether our remaining days are few or many. We must not despair but pray that God will give us a faith that remains unshaken by this tragic act, that God will give us a hope that takes us to, and reaches into, the eternity of glory. With peace of heart and mind we need not fear, for a Savior is born for us, a Savior who shall bring healing to our hearts.

15 — What Shall We Say To This?

By Bob Kaul, Pastor
Olivet Lutheran Church
Fargo, North Dakota

In both of these passages from his letter to the Romans, Paul begins with a question that is probably rattling around in most of our minds this week. What then are we to say? What then are we to say about these things? What in the world has gone wrong in the world that the life of such a young man as _____ should come to such a tragic end? What shall we say? _____ was a person with many fine qualities; Paul would even call them "gifts of the Spirit." _____ had the gifts of love, patience, kindness, and gentleness. His personality overflowed with generosity and compassion. He was a happy-go-lucky guy who loved nature, who couldn't stand to see others in pain, who would have done almost anything for anyone. Yet, his life came to an end surrounded by circumstances that are so confusing and so troubling to us. What shall we say?

Let's take all of our questions, all of our confusion, and all of our pain, and bring them to holy scripture this afternoon. Here we are likely to find at least some answers, less confusion, and some balm for the hurt we feel. Let's be just as honest as we can be about our questions and our pain.

I want you to think about that passage I read from Romans chapter 8 just a few moments ago. I'll tell you what, folks, as far as I'm concerned this is one of the most powerful passages that we can find in all of scripture. Paul really has a way with words. Here he says in a beautifully clear and certain statement that the love and grace of God are more powerful than anything else in the whole universe.

Paul lists his own questions right along side our own. He gets right down to the basic questions of life and death. "If God is for us, who is against us? Who shall bring any charge against God's elect? If it is God who justifies, who is to condemn? Who or what shall separate us from the love of Christ?"

Paul suggests a list of possibilities. "Who shall separate us from the love of Christ? Shall tribulation, or distress, or persecution, or famine, or nakedness, or peril, or sword?" He is clearly trying to list the most horrible things he can think of. What can come between us? What in all of existence has the potential of casting such a dark cloud over life that we are finally separated from the love of God in Christ Jesus our Lord?

We could add our own questions to his list, couldn't we? What seems to threaten to stand as a barrier between you and the love of Christ? Is it unemployment, bankruptcy, cancer, addiction, divorce, depression, guilt, the death of a loved one, especially by suicide? What's on your mind this afternoon as you think about that question: who shall separate us from the love of Christ? Go ahead. Add them to the list.

And then hear Paul's answer. No. Shall any of these things stop God from loving us? No. No. he says. In all these things we are more than conquerors through him who loved us. And then he adds to the list himself. "For I am sure that neither death, nor life, nor angels, nor principalities, nor things present, nor things to come, nor powers, nor height, nor depth, nor anything else in all creation, will be able to separate us from the love of God in Christ Jesus our Lord." God says no to anything that would get in the way of his love and grace.

I don't know about you, but when bad things happen in life I tend to look for who's to blame. I suppose most of us do that. Remember that passage in John 11 (17-27) when Lazarus, the brother of Mary and Martha had died? Martha said to Jesus, "Lord, if you had been here, my brother would not have died." Who's to blame here? Is all of this somehow

God's fault? Had God abandoned _____ to his feelings of despair? Who's to blame? Each of us is going to ask that question, if we haven't already. Was it my fault? Was it _____ fault? Was it your fault? Who's to blame?

Now listen. God has a word to say about all of this blaming. It's the same word that he said before. To all of our blaming God says no. Pinning down the blame is the easy way out of this situation, and frankly, it only makes matters worse.

What would happen if we just got really honest and asked the hidden question here? What about suicide? We'd really rather not talk about it, would we? It would be easier to leave that question under the rug. But it won't go away by ignoring it. Let me offer three don'ts about how to deal with what has happened.

Don't make this a family secret. Don't try to hide the facts. Rather, put that energy into trying to understand what depression and despair are all about. Such feelings are widespread in our society, and much understanding is needed.

Secondly, don't carry the burden of guilt for _____ action. No matter how sensitive you are to a person's feelings, no matter what precautions you might take, suicide is a choice that the person makes. That's what depression and despair can do.

Thirdly, don't brood over it. Don't brood over it. _____ death is a tragic and unfortunate thing. So is death from leukemia or heart disease or a car accident or dying on a battlefield. Death is tragic and unwelcome, no matter what the cause.

Now, while I want you to hear a clear word of grace and forgiveness this afternoon, I also want it to be clear that the church in no way promotes suicide. Nor do we promote cancer or drunk driving or war. On the contrary, we want to do everything in our power to prevent these things, everything in our power to enhance the quality and the joy of life.

The point is this. It is not for us to stand in judgment. "If it is God who justifies, who is to condemn?" It is not for us to stand in judgment. It is for us to stand in grace. God says no to all of our blaming and condemning. But God also has a powerful yes to say.

Let me refer to one more Bible passage, again from Paul. Paul had written a letter to his congregation in Corinth, promising to come and pay them a visit. But he had gotten tangled up with other problems and had to change his travel plans. This made the folks in Corinth mad and they accused Paul of being wishy washy. They even went to the extent of calling into question the gospel that he had preached. So Paul wrote back and tried to explain the situation, and he defends the gospel. In the first chapter of 2 Corinthians he says, "As surely as God is faithful, our word to you has not been yes and no. For the Son of God, Jesus Christ, whom we preached among you, was not yes and no; but in him it is always yes. For all the promises of God find their yes in him. That is why we utter the Amen through him, to the glory of God."

It is grace in which we stand. It is God's yes in which we stand. Let the good news of God's yes penetrate your ears and your hearts today and every day of your life. God says no to everything that would set up a barrier between you and his love, and God says yes to the forgiveness of sins, to salvation and new life.

God's yes is for you, it is for _____, it is sure, it is certain, it is unquestionable. The yes of God's grace is sufficient for this day and for every day. Amen.

16 — Death And Birth

By Henry G. Brinton, Pastor
Calvary Presbyterian Church
Alexandria, Virginia

Two things you can never predict with precision are birth and death. It was a bitter cold January night when a young woman went into labor with her first child. She grabbed her minister husband, said, "It's time," and he replied, "Okay, but first we need to stop by the funeral home." He had a funeral service scheduled for 11:00 the next morning, and he knew they'd never be finished with the delivery in time.

The minister's wife was not amused. But she got him back by complaining that the car was too hot, and insisting that they drive all the way to the hospital, through the winter night, with the windows open.

This week we're dealing with the overlap of death and birth once again. Today we gather for a funeral service for _____; tomorrow many of us will be in this same place to celebrate the birth of Jesus Christ. Our emotions are mixed: we're feeling the shock and sadness of death, as well as the anticipation and joy of birth. As we think about life without _____, grief threatens to overwhelm us but as we worship God for entering life as the Christ child, we are given new hope for days to come.

I can't help but think that this is how _____ would want us to feel. Never one to want too much attention directed toward himself, he would want us to be thinking about Jesus Christ on a day like this. Since so much of _____ life was devoted to pointing people to Christ, it seems fitting that as we thank God for _____, we also thank God for Jesus.

I was always impressed by the ways in which ＿＿＿＿＿＿＿
attempted to live out his commitment to Christ. While many
people today put their careers ahead of all else, ＿＿＿＿＿＿＿
lived as though his true calling was to serve his family, his
church, and his community. *(Here thanksgivings are given for
the deceased's character and forms of service.)*

We give thanks today for ＿＿＿＿＿＿＿ life on earth, but
we also give thanks that his life continues in God's heavenly
kingdom. His Lord and Savior Jesus Christ, whose birth we
are about to celebrate, has come again and received him into
everlasting life. "Let not your hearts be troubled," said Jesus
to his followers; "Believe in God, believe also in me. In my
Father's house are many rooms; if it were not so, would I have
told you that I go and prepare a place for you?" Because
＿＿＿＿＿＿＿ did believe in God, and in his Son, Jesus has
prepared a place for him, a place where he can be free of physical hardship and pain.

We can be thankful that unlike the disciple Thomas,
＿＿＿＿＿＿＿ did know the way to God's house. He believed
that Jesus was "the way, and the truth, and the life," and that
the way to the Father was through the Son. ＿＿＿＿＿＿＿
knew God because he knew Jesus Christ, and so much of what
he said and did was an attempt to help others know God in
Christ as well. He tried to show the love of Christ in his words
and actions, love that is patient and kind, not envious or boast-
ful or arrogant or rude. ＿＿＿＿＿＿＿ tried to be a channel
for this love that bears all things, believes all things, hopes
all things, and endures all things.

Because this love never ends, we can follow in
＿＿＿＿＿＿＿'s foot steps and attempt to be channels of love
as well. We can trust the same Lord that he trusted, the Lord
that walked with him through the valley of the shadow of
death, and we can share Christ's love as we serve our fami-
lies, churches, and communities. We will not be with
＿＿＿＿＿＿＿ until we see him, face to face, in God's kingdom, but until that time we can carry on his loving service.

_____ knew that both birth and death are important parts of Christian life. The beginning of life is joyful, but so is the transition to everlasting life with God. Everything we encounter as Christian — even death — should be illuminated by the light of resurrection. When we adore the babe of Bethlehem this Christmas, let's look for more than a beautiful child: let's look for Christ on the cross, and for our resurrected Lord. The baby born in our hearts again this week is the Son of God who leads us to eternal life.

Birth and death will go on forever, surprising us and shocking us. Funerals will overlap with deliveries, and loved ones will die during Christmas week. Fortunately, as Christians we can believe that birth and death both lead to new life, because our God is with us not only in life, but in death, and in life beyond death.

May the Lord of death and life bless you all as we celebrate the new life of Christ. This life is with us now, as we enjoy the Christmas season, and it is with _____, as he enjoys everlasting life. Amen.

17 — Resurrection And Life

By Jonathan W. Schriber, Senior Pastor
St. Johns Lutheran Church
Sidney, Ohio

I was very anxious to meet _____. Even before my ministry here, I knew a bit of the _____ legacy through my close relationship with Pastor _____. Upon arriving here, I was reminded of this man's impact on the life of this congregation. I wanted to meet his widow — both as a link to him and yet in her own right as a person, a wife, a mother.

_____ now rests from her labors in the presence of her Lord. We gather, sorrowful that she is separated from us, but rejoicing in her life she had and celebrating her resurrection through Jesus Christ our Lord.

_____ is at home in heaven, not because she was married to Rev. _____, not because she was a faithful wife, a loving mother, not because she was a dedicated, hardworking member of the church, not because of faithful service alongside her husband, not because of any legacy.

She lives because of the words of Jesus to an earlier servant and sister — Martha — "I am the resurrection and the life." Because of Christ she lives, because of Christ we celebrate, because of Christ — we too shall live.

"I am the resurrection and the life" said Jesus — what power, what hope, what joy! Right now, here, this moment, Jesus says that to you, to me. In this little insignificant corner of the world, Christ comes to us with his comfort, his love, his life!

Have you ever noticed though how some of the most fundamental words Jesus first shares with the world are considered unimportant, insignificant? Remember what Jesus said to the Samaritan woman at Jacob's well — "The water that I give him will become in him a spring of water welling up to eternal life." And then later his word, admitting he is the Messiah, "I who speak to you am he."

His words to the man who was born blind and was sitting alongside the road, "I am the light of the world." And then his words to Nicodemus in the nocturnal meeting, "Unless one is born of water and the Spirit he cannot enter the kingdom of God."

Here in our text, it was just Jesus and Martha. Oh, to be sure, many others were standing around, in earshot of Jesus, but it was Martha in her sorrow and pain crying out. Not in anger, just sorrow — "only if you had been here," followed immediately by her statement of faith — not in desperation, but faith, "and even now I know what ever you ask from God ..."

And to Martha, Jesus said, "I am the resurrection and the life." To her, to the world, to you and to me, he said, he died, he rose — I am the resurrection and the life. For Martha, Mary, Lazarus, for _____, for you and me, Jesus — the resurrection and the life — our life.

As if you or I were the only one to be saved, he came. You know, the president belongs to all Americans, the queen to all the British, yet no one can really claim them in a personal or intimate way. But Jesus is ours, he comes to us in a very real, very personal very powerful way.

In the midst of your pain, sorrow, frustrations, decisions, family strife, financial stress, addiction, fears, joys, happiness, family times — in the midst of all of life Christ came for you, to give you power, to set you free from sin, death and the devil. He came to give you abundant life!

"I am the resurrection and the life; he who believes in me, though he dies, yet shall he live, and whoever lives and believes in me shall never die." Do we really grasp the power and magnitude of these words? As one scholar once said, "A passage so majestic and unfathomable, has the quality of music rather than words."

At times, we get so wrapped up in the ways, the messages, the priorities of the world, that the message of Christ is lost. We live in a society, a time where we speak of grabbing all the gusto you can, you only go around once, do your own thing, life is short — so do what you have to to be happy. We speak of death as an escape from the pressure of life, or as the loss of a loved one.

I would hope no one here today considers the life of _____ as lost. She is very much found, in the grace, the protection of her Lord. We are separated from her, but she is not lost. And life is much more than grabbing gusto — life is to be intimately connected with our Creator, with our Lord and Savior. Christ wants us to live life to the fullest — to be sure — but full of a gospel sense — filled with the Spirit, with the grace, the forgiveness, the love, the power of God.

I dare say, even if Jesus had not raised Lazarus from the grave, his words to Martha would have remained as powerful. For Lazarus would die again, but now for Martha and for the others and for us, through Christ — life here and now takes on purpose and meaning.

Martha would never be the same again. No matter what would come her way, no matter what would happen — Christ would be with her, she would have life.

It is the power of the resurrection that changes all of life. Look at the difference it made in the lives of people following Christ's resurrection. All the powers of evil and darkness had been destroyed. The skirmishes continue, but the victory has been won — for _____, for you, for me.

The early followers of Christ faced great persecution, great periods of trial and tribulation and brutal death. But in Christ, there was no fear. There was life — life now committed to Christ — life eternal. Even though death would still claim the flesh, life would continue, and even the body will be raised.

As we gather this day to remember, to give thanks to God for _____ and to celebrate her life, we can also give thanks for the example she has left us — as Martha — a faithful servant of the Lord, one who lived in the power of this word, this promise.

Each time we had worship and celebrated communion, _____ was there if she could be. Each time with eagerness she reached out her hand to receive in the body and blood of her Lord that new life, that power, that forgiveness, that love. She eagerly listened to God's word as it was read and proclaimed — clinging to that which was so precious.

We would do well to so treasure these gifts. To truly embrace what these words mean to us for daily life, and for life eternal. To know that each day Christ walks with us, that each day we are empowered to be faithful witnesses to the gospel, to know each day our salvation is secure through the cross and empty tomb of Jesus Christ.

Dear friends in Christ, we are here this day, this hour to remember, to thank God, to celebrate new life. The life that is _____ now, in the fullest and grandest sense, the life that is ours — all through Jesus the Christ.

In these final days of Lent, as we are vividly reminded of the passion of our Lord we take to us the tremendous price of our redemption, and can only love him more. And in the power of the cross, our sins were paid for, our lives bought with the precious blood of the Lamb. He who said to Martha — I am the resurrection and the life — gave his life that we might live.

I am the resurrection and the life — this year, Easter came a little early for _____. Amen.

18 — Like Abraham To The Slaughter

By Dennis E. Dinger, Pastor
Hope United Methodist Church
Canal Winchester, Ohio

It is not good for us to be here. There is something wrong, there is something almost obscene, about parents being at their own child's funeral. We are hurt beyond grief by the suddenness and by the waste of _____ death and we need to talk about that. We want to shake our fists at the sky and curse God for the unfairness of the burden he has given us and we need to talk about that. We wonder how we will ever get through this day, and how we will get through tomorrow, and if we will ever smile again and we need to talk about that.

We need to talk, but I am as speechless as you. I feel drained by the crying and the mourning of the past days; I feel, as you do, desolated by thoughts of the loneliness that lies ahead. I say with the psalmist, "My God, my God, why have you forsaken me?" And God answered me by saying, "Let me tell you a story." This is the story God told: God tested Abraham, God said to Abraham, "Take your son, your only son Isaac, whom you love and go to the region of Moriah. Sacrifice him there as a burnt offering on one of the mountains I will tell you about." And Abraham did as the Lord commanded. When they reached the place God had told him about, Abraham built an altar ... reached for the knife to slay his son. But the angel of the Lord called out to him from heaven, "Do not lay a hand on the boy. Now I know that you fear God, because you have not withheld from me your son."

That is a painful story, I know. Painful because its details so closely parallel the manner of _____ death; and

61

doubly painful because God spared Isaac and did not spare _____. Nevertheless this is the story that God has left us, and if we would speak as Christians about _____ death, we must come to grips with it as Abraham had to come to grips with the possibility of Isaac's death.

The story of Abraham and Sarah and Isaac — the story of _____ and _____ and _____ — compels us to face the reality of parenthood: the possibility that we might lose our child, and the question of our willingness to risk so much love against so great a loss.

_____, so far as this world goes, you have lost _____. He died in an accident in a profession where accidents are common. He died, as we see it, too young, with too many dreams unfulfilled, with too many hopes unrealized. If only, we want to say, he could have lived to 40, or 60; if only, we think, he could have done this or seen that; if only, if only ... if only, from this day forth, will be part of the litany of our lives. Yet _____ had already achieved his greatest ambition: he was a good son. And you had achieved your greatest goal: you were good parents. _____ died, and nothing can change that, but he died in the fullness of his health, in the spring of his manhood, and his last moments were spent doing what he loved more than anything in the world, he was farming with his dad. If only _____ had lived to 120, he could not have been happier or more fulfilled, more proud of himself or more a joy to you, than he was that last bright morning of his life.

The possibility of death is the reality of life. To face that possibility, with our hands turned cheerfully to our work, with our hearts open to others, with the certain knowledge that we have loved and been loved — that is the test of life, and _____ passed that test with flying colors.

We have a test to take and to pass as well. Remember how our story began? God tested Abraham. God is testing _____, and all of us who knew _____ and loved him: our test is whether we can accept that God loves him even more; that God is taking care of _____, and that God is even now taking care of us.

_____ is not alone. The Bible tells us that the saints are gathered around the throne of God. _____ is there, surrounded by people he knows, and waiting for us. The Bible says that while we wait, we are surrounded by a cloud of witnesses.

And so we are. Within an hour of the accident, everyone at our church knew about it and were doing what they could to help. By evening our entire community knew, and everyone pitched in to help with the milking, to bring food, to sit and visit, to hug and cry and remember and mourn together. And we will be here, with you, and for you, as long as you need us. Out of our common weakness and helplessness, God will give us the strength to carry on.

_____ was a fine man. He was a good Christian. He was a skilled farmer. He was a loving son, and a devoted brother. If you regret all the things you did not get to say to him on that last day, be comforted by the thought that everything important you had to say, you said with every word, with every gesture, with every moment you had together in these 20 years. There was nothing of your love, or of your pride, or of your hopes and dreams, that _____ did not know. And be comforted by the knowledge that _____ lived the values you taught so faithfully that anyone who knew him knew you, and was proud to know you both.

I have heard a father cry out, "My son is dead." I have heard a mother scream, "My baby is gone." I have seen a sister racked with sobs, and watched a brother struggle to contain himself. And I have anguished with them, as so many of you have done. But above the sounds of our shared grief, I have heard another voice, and I would have his words be the last words to you: "Blessed are the dead who die in the Lord; Yea, saith the Spirit, that they may rest from their labors; and their works do follow them."

Our beloved _____, rest well from your labors. God loves you. We love you. And we will be with you again.

19 — The Circle Of Life

By Charles R. Leary, M. Div.
Episcopal Clergyman
Medway, Ohio

Life has brought us full circle again!

I want you to visualize a circle. It might be your ring, or the circle in the cross (pointing to the Celtic cross above the altar). I use the word, circle, because I feel that deep inside God's universe there is no real beginning and no real ending. There are continuous circles marked by all kinds of events, some natural, some traumatic, some glorious, and some just ordinary. Some we plan, some happen, some we memorialize. But all in all, we call them beginnings and endings by the nature of them.

Birth we call a beginning. Death we call an end. Marriage we call a beginning. Divorce we call an end.

But think about it. One event can be both a beginning and an end. Retirement. An end? Actually, retirement is an end of a certain kind of activity in life, but marks a beginning of a new kind of activity in life. _____ retired from government service but he could not let himself give up on work. So he assumed a more relaxed job, a shoe salesman part-time. After a while age and health affected him severely and further altered his participation in life.

_____, known to his family and colleagues as _____, had his beginning in this life 85 years ago. _____ ... baptismal name, _____, was born _____. On Sunday morning, _____, he made his exit from this life.

_____ leaves memories in all who have known him as husband, father, brother, friend and colleague. Those memories will remain for as long as we choose to nurture them.

The only way we Christians know how to deal with death is in terms of the resurrection. Hence I say, circle of life, because death is not the end, only the exit from this life to another.

Each of us is somewhere in that circle.

One matures, graduates, loves, follows a career through successes and failures, and lives through pleasures and pain. And, of course, we are here because someone chose to marry, have a family, and experience the enrichment, sometimes disappointment, that brings. Each of these choices and life-adventures is a circle within the larger cosmic circle of God's universe.

Each time we complete a circle — graduate, fall in love, become parents, complete a career in retirement, lose a loved one in death, become a believer — in each of these we assess where we have been and do some planning about where we go next. That's the way we put meaning and fulfillment into the circle, and circles, of life.

Always in an effort to save ourselves from confusion and from going adrift in the sea of life it seems natural to ask questions. Who am I, anyway? Why am I here? What are the factors that linked me up with the people who are so important in my life? Am I grateful? Am I telling those with whom I am connected that I am grateful? Am I telling those near and dear to me that I need them, and am I being the kind of person they need?

Some of the questions may have no answers, or if they do, the answer changes from time to time. But each time we ask them and ponder them they tend to bring us back to center and give us a sense of direction. And in the end, our lives become our answer to those questions. That is the essence of making the circle complete.

Someone expressed it in verse:

People come into our lives
And walk with us a mile.
And then — because of circumstances
Only stay a while.
They fill a need within
The days move quickly by!
And then they're gone —
Beyond our reach.
We often wonder why!
God only knows the reason
Why we meet
And share a smile.
Why people come into our lives
And walk with us a mile. — Source unknown

When I read the newspaper and watch television, I see that faith and hope have a lot of subtle enemies: gloom and doom, pessimism, depression, disillusionment, boredom, fear. Negativism — lack of faith, lack of hope — is the rich seedbed for indifference, insecurity, protectionism, and self-imposed and fantasy-based guilt trips.

A lot of people give up on life; they resign and let themselves become victims to life's circumstances. A lot of people reject God because they are unable to see purpose shining through the chaos, disorder, disaster, pain and suffering that life brings.

How can we cut through the gloom and doom stuff? I suggest two guidelines: One, treat life as if 10 percent is what happens and 90 percent is how to manage it. And two, I know that life is not easy, but I cling to the victory that Jesus claimed, "In the world you will have trouble, but never lose heart — I have conquered the world."

I invite you to join me in affirming the faith that _____ believed and practiced in The Apostles' Creed.

Seamstress
Ecclesiastes 3:7a

20 — Of Thimbles And Thread

By Lawrence H. Craig, Pastor
St. Paul's United Church of Christ
Hermitage, Pennsylvania

_____ was a seamstress. Such talent was hers as a hobby. Such talent was hers in her labors beyond those of a homemaker. _____ wasn't one for buying cloth, cutting out patterns, or creating clothing to wear. Instead, she was one who took clothing that was already sewn. Clothing that needed to be changed when the sizes and styles in people's lives changed. Simply put, _____ altered fashions, which didn't fit. _____ repaired articles and items that were torn and tattered, thus giving them new life.

Removing the stitching, she took clothing apart. Snipping and clipping its material, she reworked the garment. Then, with precision and patience; using skill and love, relying on needle, thimble and thread, _____ rejoined and reunited the cloth fragments and pieces. Under her expert care the clothing became whole again; useful again. The garments she altered took on new and functional life once more. A good seamstress like _____ can look at clothing and tell if quality is present. A good seamstress examining a garment knows if its seams are secure or if its patterns are in place.

This morning we gather to celebrate and to remember before God the life of _____. We come with heavy hearts. We come having inward pain and displaying outward sorrow. Yet, we come knowing that the God of our faith, the God of comfort, support and healing love is present in the midst of death and is present in our midst this day. Like a

good seamstress, God knows that because of _____
death the quality of your life has been diminished. God knows the seams which hold your emotions together are on this day less secure. God knows that the pattern of your days, once orderly, is now out of place.

_____ has died. Life has been changed. No matter how we view death, or how determined we are to accept her death, it just does not fit. Her death is so unexpected, so untimely. The garment of grief is not what God intends for us to wear. Yet it is a part of the wardrobe of life. It is what is worn by you this day. Grief is unfair, uncomfortable, unwanted. It leaves you hurting. You ask, what are you to do? How are you to handle this? You must look to your faith, for it is faith that tells us we are to turn to God. We are not people without hope. In God is where your hope is found and where your healing shall begin.

God is much like the seamstress. Just as persons turned to _____ for alterations when clothing failed to fit, you need to turn to God now. God has the ability to make the kind of alternations your lives now need. God can do what is necessary for you to become renewed and functional in life again. God can take the torn pieces and fragmented fabric of your lives, and like a good seamstress, God can mend the fabric of your life. God, with expert care, can return security to your emotions, restore order to the pattern of your days, and renew quality to your life. With God, all things are possible.

Just as _____, using needle, thimble and thread, altered clothing, so it could be reworked, made whole and became renewed again, God's message during this current Advent season offers you hope in your despair; peace to settle your unrest; love to overcome your angered confusion and joy to replace your inward pain and outward sorrow. God's Advent has the power to bring renewal and restoration to broken and fragmented lives. May you feel God's presence, experience God's closeness, sense God's peace and receive new life.

21 — Welcome To The Banquet

By Barbara G. Schmitz, Rector
St. Margaret's Episcopal Church
Hazel Park, Michigan

On the night before Jesus died, he gathered with his friends in an upper room. In that sacred space, three things happened that Christians have remembered and celebrated ever since.

First, Jesus got up from the table. He took off his outer garment, and put on a towel. He put on the clothing of a servant. Scripture tells us that he could do this because "he knew that he had come from God and was going to God." In other words, he knew who he was, and what he was about.

Then Jesus poured water into a wash basin and began, one by one, to wash the disciples' feet. When he got to Peter, Peter refused. "No," he said, "you're not going to wash my feet." Jesus insisted. Peter gave in.

A Japanese Christian named Koyama has suggested that when we die, Jesus will be with us as he was on this last night before he died. He will be waiting for us with a towel tied 'round his waist. He, the master, the ruler of the universe, will be on bended knee awaiting us. He will pour water into a basin. He will offer to wash our feet and wipe them with a towel. He will look deeply inside us.

Jesus will ask, "You've had a difficult journey, haven't you? You must be exhausted and dirty. Let me wash your hands and your feet. Let me be your servant."

The second thing that happened on this special night was that Jesus gave them a new commandment, a new mandate, which is why we call this night "Maundy (or mandate) Thursday."

69

Jesus said to them, "If I, your Teacher, have washed your feet, you also ought to wash one another's feet. For I have set you an example, that you also should do as I have done to you."

What does it mean to die and enter the nearer presence of our Savior? What does it mean to spend eternity in heaven? It means a place where people act as servants toward one another.

There is an old story about a fellow who visited a town. There was a large pot of stew, large enough to feed everyone in town, and the smell was delicious, but around the pot sat desperate, starving people. They all had spoons with very long handles which reached into the pot, but because the spoons were longer than their arms, they couldn't get the stew into their mouths.

Then the man visited another town, just like the first one, again with a pot of stew big enough to feed everyone. The people had the same long-handled spoons, but they were all well nourished, talking away, and very content. The fellow was confused. How could this be? "It's simple," said the guide, "for they have learned to feed one another."

At our death, Jesus will invite us to live in love and servanthood toward one another for all eternity. That is what we call being in heaven.

The third thing that happened on that particular night was that Jesus took bread, gave thanks, broke it, and gave it to the disciples, saying "This is my body, which is given for you."

Then he took the wine, gave thanks, and gave it to them saying, "This is my blood which is poured out for you."

During our lives on earth, we are nourished Sunday by Sunday with the body and blood of our Lord. At our death, Jesus will welcome us to our place at the table in the heavenly kingdom. "Come," he will say, "The banquet is ready."

> And on that mountain the Lord of hosts will make for all peoples a feast of rich food, a feast of well-aged wines, of rich food filled with marrow, of well-aged wines strained clear.   — Isaiah 25:6-9

And Jesus will take bread and wine, and bless it, and sit down to feast with us in the kingdom ... as it says in Revelation,

They will hunger no more, and thirst no more; the sun will not strike them, nor any scorching heat, and he will guide them to springs of life ...

On this night, Jesus washed feet, he gave a new commandment to love one another, he fed them with his own body and blood. We who have been washed in baptism, lived in love, and been nourished by Christ's body and blood will find at our death that Christ awaits us. Christ washes our feet. Christ invites us to servanthood. And Christ will welcome us to heaven, saying, "Welcome to the banquet." Amen.

22 — Let The Children Come To Me

**By Mary Venema Swierenga, Associate Pastor
Vienna Presbyterian Church
Vienna, Virginia**

_____ graced this earth for three months and four days. Not a long time at all when compared to the biblical span of three-score and 10 years. Three months and four days is not a long enough time. They'll agree: three months and a few days is too short. Too short for _____ to learn to walk and talk, to read and ride a bike. That's part of our pain as we mourn _____ too-soon death: we expect and assume that children will flourish and grow, but _____ life was too short for that to do anything more than begin to happen. A child's death is a reversal of expectations. And so we grieve.

But he didn't live too short a time to establish himself as a well-loved little boy with a personality all his own. _____, his sister is — according to _____ and _____ — a ball of fire, one who has asserted herself strongly since day one. _____ seemed a gentler spirit. Not that he wasn't a fighter — He'd managed to come home from the neo-natal intensive care unit of the hospital, overcoming many of the tremendous odds against a baby born prematurely. "A tough little guy" is the way his dad describes him.

_____ lived long enough to evoke a lot of love, long enough to acquire those silly, endearing, cherished nicknames we parents and grandparents give to our babies as we hold them, loving them so much that we resort to baby talk because adult language cannot fully contain or express the emotions that infants arouse in us. "Little man." "You old goat." "Peanut." This little boy with all these names got to where he smiled, and laughed little baby laughs, and followed people around with his eyes and gave them lots of joy. Many people were praying that _____ would make it. But after three months and four days his valiant heart gave out, and he died. Part of our pain is that, while his life was too short, it was long enough for us to come to love him and so we grieve, missing him.

But we do not grieve as those who have no hope. For _____ is now with God. He now has a body that works. He has no need to struggle for breath any more. He lives in heaven in a way that he — and none of us — could live on earth.

In the gospel of Matthew we have the episode where the disciples would have kept the children away from Jesus, lest they bother him. Jesus disagreed with them. "Let the children come to me," he said. "Do not try to stop them; for the kingdom of heaven belongs to such as these." And he laid his hands on them and blessed them.

The hope of coming to be with God, blessed by Jesus, is held forth for all who are children — the children of God. For us children of God it is still a hope. For _____, one of God's little children, that hope is now a reality. "Let the children come to me," Jesus invites. _____ has come.

But we are still here — the children of God who stand facing this death, alternating between faith and tears, between trust and lament. Psalm 42 is a lament in the context of a faith that endures. The psalmist — a child of God, a man of faith — goes back and forth between trust and lament. "My tears have been my food day and night," he says. And remembers what it was like when life was more joyful: when "I went with the throng, and led them in procession to the house of God, with glad shouts and songs of thanksgiving." But now it's different, he says: "My soul is cast down within me." But then he knows that his faith is not dead, for he discovers he can still say, "Hope in God, for I shall again praise him, my Savior and my God." But the grief washes over him yet again, and he laments to God his rock: "Why have you forgotten me? Why go I mourning because of the oppression of the enemy?" And again replies in faith, "Hope in God, for I shall again praise him, my Savior and my God."

_____ death is a fact, a hard and painful fact. But death does not have the last word. God has the last word, and that word is life. God loves us and gives us life. "I am the resurrection and the life," Jesus says. Life is found in God's Son Jesus, and it begins in this life and is perfected in the next.

_____ has perfect life now. And because we can believe that by faith, we can go back and forth between lament and faith as we mourn and miss this precious child, knowing all the while that our hope is in God, our God and our Savior, who loves us always and gives us life. Thanks be to God! Amen.